# FRANCE

## BOB PROSSER

Evans

## TITLES IN THE COUNTRIES OF THE WORLD SERIES:
## BRAZIL • FRANCE • JAPAN • KENYA • UNITED KINGDOM • USA

Published by Evans Brothers Limited
2A Portman Mansions
Chiltern Street
London W1U 6NR

VISIT OUR WEBSITE
www.evansbooks.co.uk

Produced for Evans Brothers Limited by
Monkey Puzzle Media,
Gissing's Farm, Fressingfield
Suffolk IP21 5SH

First published 2002
© copyright Evans Brothers 2002
© copyright in the text Bob Prosser 2002

**British Library Cataloguing in Publication Data**
Prosser, Bob
France. - (Countries of the world)
1.France - Juvenile literature
I.Title
944

914.4

ISBN 0 237 52266 7

Editor: Polly Goodman
Designer: Jane Hawkins
Map artwork by Peter Bull
Charts and graph artwork by Encompass Graphics Ltd
All photographs are by Dorian Shaw except: *Airbus* 40-41;
*Corbis* 27 Jonathan Blair; *Corbis Digital Stock* front endpapers,
title page, imprint & contents, 60, 61, back endpapers.

**Endpapers (front):** A café terrace in Paris.
**Title page:** The Louvre Pyramid in Paris.
**Imprint and Contents page:** The Arc de
Triomphe, Paris.
**Endpapers (back):** The River Seine and the
Pont (bridge) Royale, Paris.

# CONTENTS

INTRODUCING FRANCE      8

LANDSCAPE AND CLIMATE      10

POPULATION      20

AGRICULTURE      28

INDUSTRY      34

LEISURE AND TOURISM      42

URBAN FRANCE      46

TRANSPORT, ENERGY AND THE ENVIRONMENT      52

GLOSSARY      58

FURTHER INFORMATION      59

INDEX      60

The French flag is called the *tricolor*, or 'three-coloured'. Red and blue represent the city of Paris and white is the traditional colour for French kings.

# INTRODUCING FRANCE

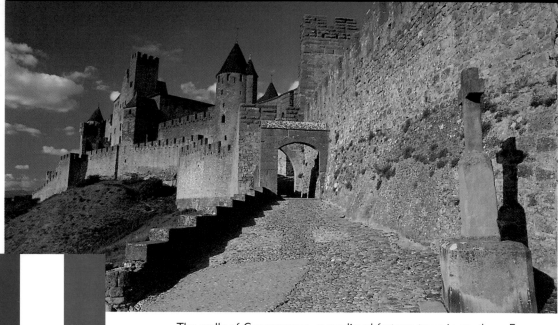

The walls of Carcassonne, a medieval fortress town in southern France.

France is the largest country in Western Europe. It lies along the western edge of the European continent, with extensive coastlines along the Atlantic Ocean and the Mediterranean Sea. The Mediterranean island of Corsica is part of France, although it is demanding greater political freedom from the mainland.

France has a long history as an independent country with its own government. Over the centuries it has had to defend this independence, enduring two invasions within the past 100 years. Its long cultural heritage has given France a rich variety of historic towns surrounded by rural landscapes. Its heritage has also created great national pride. Yet there are also strong contrasts between the regions, which can be seen most clearly in the styles of buildings, language and dialects, dress and customs, and food and drink in different parts of the country.

## KEY DATA

| | |
|---|---|
| Area: | 549,100km² |
| Population: | 59.1 million (2000) |
| Capital City: | Paris |
| Currency: | Euro (€) (since Jan 2002) |
| GDP per Capita: | US$22,897* |
| Highest Point: | Mt Blanc (4,807m) |

*Calculated on Purchasing Power Parity basis
Source: World Bank

## A MULTICULTURAL SOCIETY

France once had an extensive empire. For example, Algeria, Morocco and Vietnam were all French colonies. This helps to explain the large numbers of immigrants from these countries living in France today. Over the past 40 years, the country has attracted many thousands of immigrants and refugees from southern, central and Eastern Europe, looking for jobs and safety. As a result, France today is a truly multicultural society. A majority of the population belong to the Catholic faith, but there are many other religions.

## THE EUROPEAN UNION

For more than 200 years, France has been a republic. In 1957, it became one of the first countries to join the European Community, which later became the European Union (EU). Today, in cooperation with Germany, it is a strong supporter of greater European integration. In area, it is the largest EU country. Its population is approximately the same as that of the UK and Italy, but less than Germany's 80 million. It is one of the richest countries of the EU, with a modern agricultural and industrial structure.

France, including the island of Corsica, is divided into 22 regions (see map below) and

The traditional game of boules is a street form of bowls and part of the distinctive French culture.

96 departments. Each department is made up of a number of *cantons*, which contain *communes*, the smallest administrative units.

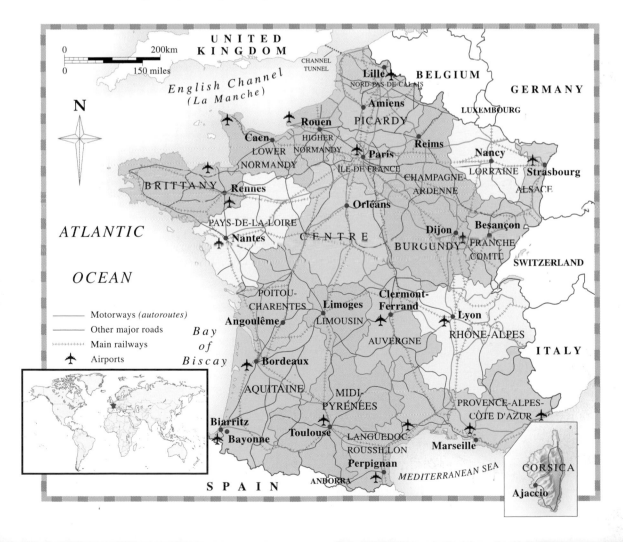

# LANDSCAPE AND CLIMATE

Rolling farming landscape in the Garonne valley, part of the Aquitaine Basin in south-west France.

France can be divided into three main physical regions: plains and valleys, old uplands and young fold mountains. There are several examples of each type of region across the country. The mountainous island of Corsica is a separate region.

## PLAINS AND VALLEYS

These are lowland regions that are mostly below 300m. They are flat or gently rolling landscapes, with occasional steep hills and ridges. The lowlands vary in shape and character. There are two broad basins, the Paris and Aquitaine basins, which are crossed by major rivers. In contrast, there are two long, river lowlands, the Rhône-Saone and Rhine valleys, fringed by hills and mountains. Finally there is a narrow strip of lowland along the Mediterranean coast.

## PARIS AND AQUITAINE BASINS

The Paris and Aquitaine basins are large plains into which the main rivers and their tributaries have cut wide valleys. They extend across much of northern and western France and cover one-third of the total land area.

The Paris Basin has the Seine River flowing through the middle. In the east and south-east there is a series of escarpments, such as the Île-de-France scarp east of Reims. The escarpments are formed from sandstone and limestone, which run under much of the Paris Basin. This region has deep, well-drained and fertile soils.

A popular surfing beach in the Landes, on the coast of the Bay of Biscay.

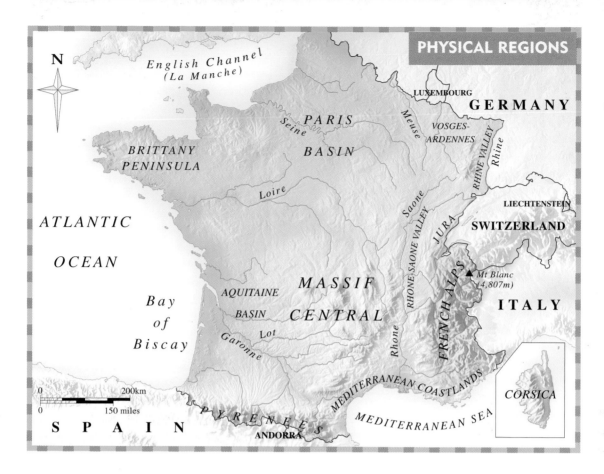

N

*English Channel
(La Manche)*

LUXEMBOURG

GERMANY

*Seine* PARIS
BASIN

*Meuse*

VOSGES-
ARDENNES

*Loire*

RHINE VALLEY

*Rhine*

BRITTANY
PENINSULA

ATLANTIC

OCEAN

*Saone*

LIECHTENSTEIN

JURA

SWITZERLAND

RHONE-SAONE VALLEY

Mt Blanc
(4,807m)

B a y
o f
B i s c a y

AQUITAINE

BASIN

MASSIF

CENTRAL

*Lot*

*Garonne*

FRENCH ALPS

ITALY

*Rhone*

0          200km
0          150 miles

MEDITERRANEAN COASTLANDS

CORSICA

S P A I N

P Y R E N E E S

ANDORRA

MEDITERRANEAN SEA

The northern parts of the Aquitaine Basin are similar to the Paris Basin, with limestone underlying gently sloping plains. Further south the rocks are covered by a blanket of sediment deposited by glaciers and rivers over the past 2 million years. There are large areas of fertile soils. The Garonne and the Lot rivers cut into the soft deposits. Along the Atlantic coast a 200km stretch of sand dunes has developed between Bordeaux and Biarritz. Known as the Landes, this is one of Europe's largest dune systems. A series of shallow lagoons called *étangs* exists behind this dune barrier.

## VALLEYS

The Rhône-Saone Valley runs north to south in a straight line. This is the result of faults that have dropped the valley floor down between the mountains on either side. The valley is broad and flat, up to 5km wide in places. The section of the Rhine Valley that is in France is similar: steep, faulted sides with a flat valley floor.

## MEDITERRANEAN COASTAL LOWLANDS

The Mediterranean coastal lowlands generally extend less than 25km from the coast. They are flat, with a number of shallow lagoons that have developed behind low sand-spits. In the past there were marshes and wetlands, but most have been drained for agriculture.

St Tropez is one of a string of famous holiday resorts along the warm, sunny Mediterranean coast.

# OLD UPLANDS

The uplands contain the oldest rock types in France and are the eroded remains of much higher mountain ranges. They vary in height: for example the Brittany Peninsula is much lower and less rugged than the Massif Central. However, they all consist of rolling plateaux cut through by steep river valleys.

## BRITTANY PENINSULA

The Brittany Peninsula is a rolling plateau of mostly ancient rocks, with a maximum height of 417m above sea level. The energy of the Atlantic Ocean against these resistant rocks has produced some spectacular coastal scenery, consisting of cliffs and rocks separating sandy bays and muddy inlets.

The rugged cliffs of Pointe du Raz, on the edge of the Brittany Peninsula.

## MASSIF CENTRAL

The central and northern part of the Massif Central is a dome of resistant rocks. In the past, igneous material was extruded, or squeezed out, and cooled to form hard volcanic rock. There is no volcanic activity any more, but despite erosion, old lava flows remain. The most spectacular evidence of volcanic activity is the series of steep, conical hills, such as the Monts Dore, which jut sharply above the plateau landscape. The Monts Dore form the highest point of the Massif Central, at 1,886m. They are the remains of the vents of ancient volcanoes, through which lava once flowed. The other evidence of volcanic activity is the thermal springs. Their warm, mineral-rich waters supported popular spa resorts in the nineteenth century. Today they are used for domestic heating schemes.

A number of faults break the massif into several pieces. For example, they separate the lie within France. Geologically, the Ardennes and the Vosges are similar to the northern Massif Central, although they are lower (less than 1,500m). However, they consist of a mixture of broken plateaux and sharp ridges, which make communications difficult. For instance, the Vosges Mountains separate the important economic regions of the Rhine valley and the Paris Basin. Like the Massif Central, there are coal and iron ore deposits around the fringes, for example in the industrial district of Lorraine. The Jura mountains, separated from the Vosges by the Belfort Gap, run south for 290km as far as the Rhône Valley below Lake Geneva. They consist of a series of limestone ridges fringed on the west by a broad plateau.

The remote volcanic uplands of the Monts Dore district of the Massif Central.

volcanic plateaux of the centre from the limestone uplands of the Causses in the west. Rivers such as the Tarn have carved deep gorges through these uplands. The faults have helped to create the rugged Cévennes ridges which face the Mediterranean in the south-east. They have also created basins, which have protected valuable mineral deposits, especially of coal and iron ore. Exploitation of these deposits has created several industrial districts, such as the coal industry around Millau in the south, and the iron and steel industry of Le Creusot in the north.

## THE VOSGES, ARDENNES AND JURA

The three other important uplands are the Vosges, the Ardennes, and the Jura, which lie in an arc along France's north-eastern and eastern borders. Only parts of these uplands

The severe weathering of these rocks in western Brittany shows the power of the storms that sweep in from the Atlantic Ocean.

# YOUNG FOLD MOUNTAINS

France has two high mountain ranges, the Pyrenees and the French Alps. Both have extensive areas over 2,000m, high enough for permanent snow and ice. They are geologically 'young' and are part of mountain chains that run eastwards across southern Europe into Turkey. For at least the past 100 million years, older rocks have been pushed upwards by movements of the African and European continents. As the uplift and pressures have continued, the rocks have been folded and broken by faulting into complex shapes. Erosion by water, ice and wind has added to this complexity to give spectacular sceneries of peaks and deeply carved valleys.

## THE PYRENEES

The Pyrenees are a continuous and rugged mountain range. They extend east to west over 400km, from the Bay of Biscay to the Mediterranean Sea, and form France's southern boundary with Spain. The mountains reach a maximum height of over 3,000m, with extensive areas over 2,000m. The western section consists mainly of limestone, and is generally below 1,800m. The central section is the highest and most rugged, built largely of resistant crystalline rocks. The eastern section has heights of over 2,000m and consists mainly of ridges and deeply cut stream valleys. Across the northern edges of the Pyrenees, a fringe of thick, younger sedimentary rocks slopes steadily towards the Aquitaine Basin. These rocks contain valuable natural gas deposits.

## THE ALPS

The fold mountains of the French Alps extend north to south from Lake Geneva to the Mediterranean coast, and form France's boundary with Switzerland and Italy. The Alps are the most spectacular mountain range in France, reaching 4,807m at Mt Blanc, the highest peak in Europe. The mountains are high enough to keep extensive areas of permanent snow and ice, including lengthy glaciers such as the Mer-de-Glace.

Much of the erosion in the High Pyrenees was made by glaciers, which have now disappeared.

These Alpine chalets were built for tourists, for skiing in the winter and walking in the summer.

The Alps can be divided into three main regions. In the north, hard, crystalline rocks lie under the Mt Blanc Massif. In the central zone, the mountains consist of highly folded and faulted sedimentary rocks, especially limestone and sandstone. Deep valleys are cut into these mountains, such as the long Chamonix Grenoble depression. To the west and south of these ranges runs an arc of sedimentary rocks, called the Pre-Alps. This zone runs south to Provence, where it is 60km wide and forms a series of ridges overlooking the Mediterranean Sea.

## CORSICA

This rugged Mediterranean island is 200km long, with a line of mountains running down the centre. The coasts are mainly rocky, with some beautiful bays and beaches.

The Alps are high enough for snow and ice to remain at higher altitudes all year round.

| RIVER FACTS | | |
|---|---|---|
| River | Length* | Source |
| Loire | 1,010km | South-east Massif |
| Rhône | 812km | Massif Central |
| Seine | 780km | Northern Massif |
| Garonne | 650km | Pyrenees |
| (*including tributaries) | | |

Heavy river traffic uses the Seine to travel between Paris and Le Havre.

## MAJOR RIVERS

France has four major drainage basins: the Seine, Loire, Garonne and Rhône-Saone. These large rivers are important transport routes and are linked by a network of canals. The rivers and their tributaries are vital sources of water supply. Controlling water quality is an increasing problem due to pollution from agriculture and industry.

### THE SEINE

The Seine and its tributaries drain most of the Paris Basin, on their way to the English Channel (known in France as La Manche). Below Paris, the Seine flows in a series of sweeping meanders, cut into the generally flat landscape. The river reaches the sea through a broad estuary. Under natural conditions, water levels are highest in winter and early spring. A series of barrages and locks control the flow, and regular dredging keeps the water deep enough for heavy barge traffic. Paris, Rouen and Le Havre are important ports and industrial cities located along the Seine.

### THE LOIRE

The Loire is France's longest river. The upper Loire and its main tributary, the Allier, flow north through the uplands of the Massif

The middle and lower Loire is a broad, navigable river, crossed by a number of bridges.

Central, cutting deep valleys. The lower Loire is a broad river cut into the plains and escarpments of the northern Aquitaine Basin. It reaches the Bay of Biscay through an estuary at the important naval base of St Nazaire. Water levels are highest during the winter. During hot, dry summers water levels can be low. However, the river is now controlled by dams, barrages and locks, which even out the flow. The middle and lower Loire takes heavy barge traffic to and from cities such as Nantes, Angers, Tours and Orléans.

## THE GARONNE

The Garonne's source is in the Pyrenees, where its streams are fed by snow. As a result, there are high water levels and risks of floods in late spring, when the snows melt. Heavy summer thunderstorms can have a similar effect. Dams along the upper river reduce the risk of flood and even out the flow. The main tributaries of the Garonne begin in the Massif Central and have cut spectacular gorges as they flow westwards. Further north, the Dordogne drains the north-west section of the Massif Central and joins the Garonne as it enters the long Gironde estuary, below Bordeaux. The mouth of the Garonne has been pushed northwards as the dune system of the Landes has developed. Together, the Garonne and the Dordogne drain most of the Aquitaine Basin. Boats can travel from the Garonne to the Mediterranean coastland and the lower Rhône via the Canal de Midi, although there is less traffic than on the other major rivers.

This river regulation scheme along the lower part of the Rhône controls flooding and maintains water levels for navigation.

## THE RHÔNE

The Rhône begins in Switzerland and flows west into France below Lake Geneva. Since the Rhône and its main tributaries are snow-fed, there is a long history of spring floods. A series of dams along the upper river reduce this flood risk and allow development in the valley. Between Lyon and Avignon, few stretches of the original river channel remain. Unlike the other major rivers of France, the Rhône reaches the sea through a delta. This delta, south of Avignon, is known as the Camargue and is up to 75km wide. It is an extensive wetland and important ecosystem, providing a habitat for millions of migrating birds (see case study on page 56)

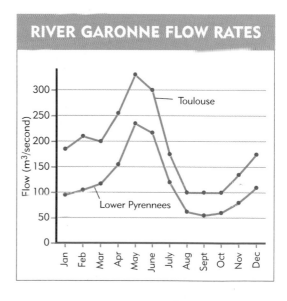

**RIVER GARONNE FLOW RATES**

Flow (m³/second) — Toulouse, Lower Pyrennees — Jan Feb Mar Apr May June July Aug Sept Oct Nov Dec

The hot summers of the warm temperate maritime region make the coasts of south-west France popular with holidaymakers.

## CLIMATE

France's size, variations in altitude and position at the western end of a major continent mean that there are a range of climates and weather conditions. Three key factors influence the local climate: the location in relation to the ocean, the latitude, and the altitude. Using these factors, France can be divided into five main climatic regions.

### COOL MARITIME TEMPERATE

This region is in the north-west, where the influence of the Atlantic Ocean means that temperatures are moderate and rarely extreme. Winters become colder to the east, away from the moderating influence of the ocean. There is a smaller temperature range between the seasons than in other regions. Most rainfall is brought by storms moving from the Atlantic. These are stronger and more frequent in the winter. As a result, most of the precipitation occurs during the winter months, some falling as snow.

### WARM TEMPERATE MARITIME

In south-west France, winters are cool but summers are hot and the temperature range between the seasons is greater than in the north because it is further south. Winter storms from the Bay of Biscay bring most rain, but thunderstorms during hot spells bring rain in the summer. Rainfall totals are lower than further north.

### COOL TEMPERATE CONTINENTAL

In north-east France, the summer heating of continental Europe and its rapid cooling in winter cause a wide seasonal temperature range. The climate is more extreme than further west: winters are colder but summers are warmer. Most rain falls during the summer, especially from irregular thunderstorms. In winter, snowfalls are common.

### MEDITERRANEAN

In southern France, the warm Mediterranean Sea, hot, tropical air moving from Africa and high levels of sunshine give the region its famous hot, dry summers. Winters are mild, although frosts do occur. Most rainfall occurs in winter, caused by storms moving west from the Atlantic. Some summer rain arrives from occasional thunderstorms.

### MOUNTAIN

The climates of the Pyrenees, Massif Central and the Alps vary widely from place to place. In general, temperatures fall as altitude

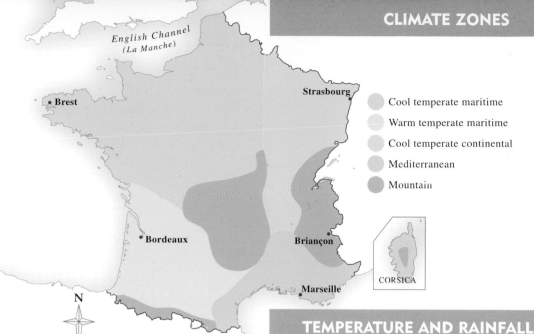

English Channel
(La Manche)

• Brest

Strasbourg

• Bordeaux

Briançon

Marseille

CORSICA

N

0          200km
0          150 miles

⬤ Cool temperate maritime
⬤ Warm temperate maritime
⬤ Cool temperate continental
⬤ Mediterranean
⬤ Mountain

increases. However, apart from the higher mountains, summers are hot. Winter temperatures are low, made cooler by frequent winds. Levels of sunshine vary according to the direction of the slopes. South-facing slopes and valleys, for example, receive more sun. Rainfall tends to be heaviest in spring and autumn, with most winter precipitation arriving as snow. Occasional summer thunderstorms may be very heavy.

At high altitudes, the Alps have a severe mountain climate with heavy winter snowfall. Summers can be warm, but snow and ice are permanent at higher altitudes.

## TEMPERATURE AND RAINFALL

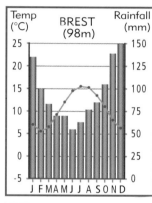

BREST (98m)

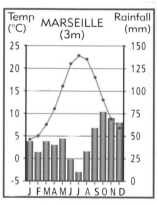

MARSEILLE (3m)

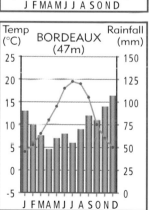

BORDEAUX (47m)

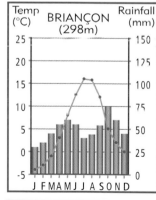

BRIANÇON (298m)

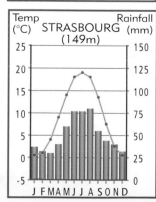

STRASBOURG (149m)

KEY:

—●—●— Temp (°C)

▌▌ Rainfall (mm)

Numbers in brackets show the city's height above sea level.

# POPULATION

Toulouse and other southern cities offer a better quality of life than some other parts of France.

In 2000 the population of France was 59.1 million, an increase of 2.9 million from 1989. This gave a population density of 108 people per km², although there were wide regional variations. In the Île-de-France region around Paris, there were more than 800 people per km², whereas in parts of the Massif Central, there were fewer than 40.

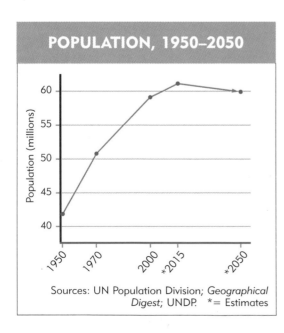

### POPULATION, 1950–2050

Sources: UN Population Division; *Geographical Digest*; UNDP.  *= Estimates

During the 1990s, the population of France grew at a rate of 0.5 per cent a year. It is forecast that between 2000–2015, the population growth will slow down to 0.2 per cent a year, giving a population of 61.1 million in 2015. The population is becoming increasingly urban, and almost one in four people now live in cities of more than 750,000 inhabitants.

The population is growing most rapidly in southern France and the Rhône-Alpes region. In contrast, the Limousin and Auvergne regions, along with some industrial districts of the north-east, have been losing population slowly. These trends are linked to economic conditions and quality of life. The government gives special help to what they call 'rural areas

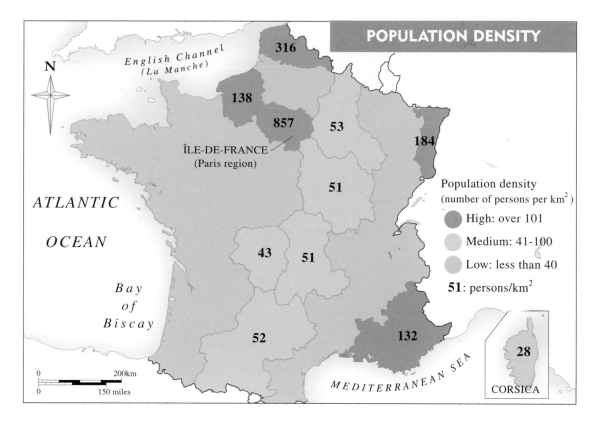

## POPULATION DENSITY

English Channel
(La Manche)

N

316

138

857

53

184

ÎLE-DE-FRANCE
(Paris region)

ATLANTIC

OCEAN

51

Population density
(number of persons per km$^2$)

High: over 101

Medium: 41-100

Low: less than 40

**51**: persons/km$^2$

43

51

Bay
of
Biscay

52

132

0          200km

0          150 miles

MEDITERRANEAN SEA

28

CORSICA

RIGHT: An increasing proportion of French
people live in large cities, many in tall
apartment blocks like these in Paris.

with development priority'. These are districts
that have been declining, but where there are
opportunities for growth.

## CAUSES OF CHANGE

As in most EU countries, the population
growth rate of France is slowing down. This is
a result of two components of change: natural
change and migration. Natural change is the
result of the balance between birth rates and
death rates. These rates are usually expressed
in numbers per 1,000 population. When birth
rates exceed death rates, there is a natural
increase in the population. When death rates
exceed birth rates, there is a natural decrease.
In 1998, the birth rate for France was 12.3
per 1,000 population, and the death rate was
9.1 per 1,000, giving a natural increase rate of
3.2 per 1,000. Over the past 30 years, this
natural increase rate has been declining.

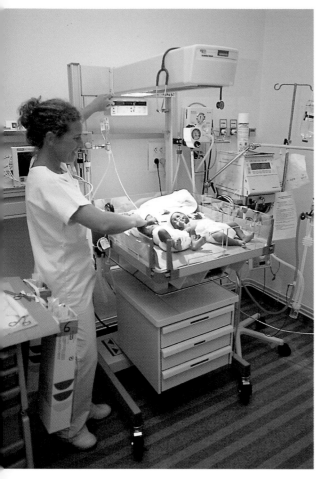

France has excellent maternity units. However, the trend is towards having fewer children.

## UNDER-FIVE MORTALITY RATE

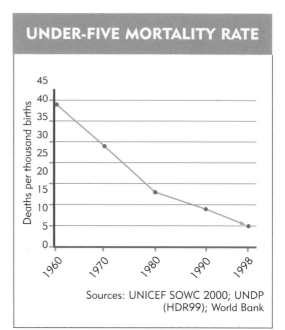

Sources: UNICEF SOWC 2000; UNDP (HDR99); World Bank

## NATURAL CHANGE

Fertility rates help to explain the decline in France's natural population growth rate and to forecast future trends. The fertility rate is the number of children a woman is likely to have during her lifetime. Assuming that births are divided evenly between boys and girls, a woman needs to have at least two children to ensure that she is replaced by one girl. This replacement level is vital if a population is to go on growing. For example, if 100 women have only 90 female children, and these daughters have the same fertility rate as their mothers, then in the longer term the population will decline. The fertility rate is below replacement level.

To sustain a population over time, fertility rates need to be at least two live births per woman. Because some female babies die young, the replacement level is usually given as 2.1. In the late 1990s, the fertility rate of France was 1.8, well below replacement level. This compares with a rate of 2.5 in 1970. So, although the under-five mortality rate is now under five per 1,000 live births, compared with nine per 1,000 in 1990, there are still not enough females in the younger age groups.

## IMMIGRATION

As rates of natural increase and fertility rates decline, the migration balance becomes increasingly important. Although thousands of people emigrate each year, France has a large net immigration balance. This means that more people move into the country than emigrate out of it. For example, during the 1990s, between 40,000 and 50,000 more people moved to France than emigrated each year. In 1998, there were 2.4 million immigrants from non-EU countries living in France, more than 4 per cent of the population. This figure compares with 4.3 million in Germany and 1.3 million in the UK.

Asian food shops such as this one in Toulouse serve the multicultural population of France.

France has a long history of immigration, which makes it a multi-ethnic, multicultural society today. Approximately one in four French citizens has at least one parent or grandparent who was an immigrant. Over the past 50 years, immigrants have come from three main regions. The largest group, making up 40 per cent of all immigrants, came from North Africa, especially Algeria and Morocco.

Both of these countries are former French colonies. The second region has been southern and Eastern Europe, mainly Italy, Poland and Romania. The third group has moved from South-east Asia, especially Vietnam, which is another ex-colony, with smaller numbers of immigrants from the Philippines and Sri Lanka.

Algerians are the largest immigrant group in France. These two workers live in Aix-en-Provence.

## ECONOMIC IMMIGRANTS

The majority of immigrants move to France for economic reasons, seeking jobs and an improved quality of life. They have provided an important labour force as the numbers of young French people have declined. Many immigrants arrived with temporary work permits. Some have obtained citizenship, but large numbers remain illegally. Most immigrants have settled in larger industrial cities. More than one in every three live in the Paris and Marseille regions, for example, and 10 per cent of the population of Marseille are immigrants, mostly from Algeria. Other large communities are found in Lyon and Toulouse.

Over recent years, the rising numbers of immigrants have caused problems, especially in some of the large, urban housing estates.

Large numbers of immigrants from Eastern Europe find work in the booming construction industry.

Also, during the 1990s, increasing numbers of political migrants, such as refugees and asylum seekers from Eastern Europe and the Balkans, have arrived. As a result of these increasing pressures and problems, the French government has introduced stricter immigration controls and it is now more difficult to obtain a work permit. Yet France has a labour shortage. The government estimates that over the next decade, the country will need up to 150,000 extra workers each year. People from other EU countries can move to France to work, but France is still likely to need immigrants from further afield.

Millions of people have moved from France's inner cities to suburban housing estates.

## INTERNAL MIGRATION

When people move homes and change jobs, it changes the population distribution of a country. Over the past 30 years, there have been five main trends of internal migration in France:

1. Movement away from the older industrial districts in north-east France.
2. Movement away from the more remote rural areas in regions such as the Massif Central and the Pyrénées.
3. Slower but continued population growth around Paris.
4. Short-distance moves from inner cities to the edges of cities and surrounding towns.
5. Increasing migration to the south-west and south of France, where new industries are locating and there are high-quality environments.

# POPULATION STRUCTURE

One of the most important trends in the French population is that it is 'ageing', which means increasing numbers of people are in the older age groups. By 1998, more than one in every five people were over 60 years of age. This 'top-heavy' population structure can be seen in the country's age-sex pyramid (right).

A major factor influencing this trend is the increase in life expectancy. French people are living longer now than ever before. Between 1970 and 1998, the average life expectancy for men rose from 68.4 to 74.6 years; for

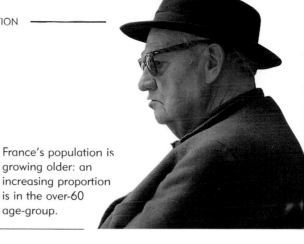

France's population is growing older: an increasing proportion is in the over-60 age-group.

women the increase was from 75.9 to 82.2 years. Combined with falling birth rates and fertility rates, it is possible to forecast that the population structure will continue to 'age', and in the future, the population may begin to decline unless immigration remains high.

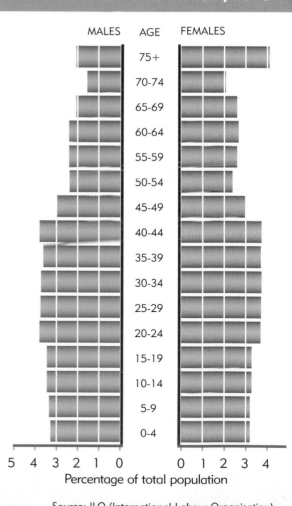

**FRANCE POPULATION, 1998**

MALES     AGE     FEMALES

Percentage of total population

Source: ILO (International Labour Organisation)

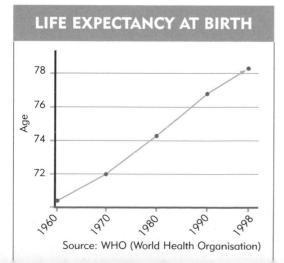

**LIFE EXPECTANCY AT BIRTH**

Source: WHO (World Health Organisation)

# THE PYRÉNÉES REGION

The Pyrénées region is an excellent example of what is happening in rural France, especially the more remote areas. The six departments that cover the Pyrénées and their northern fringes have a total population of approximately 495,000. The population density is low – only 36 people per km² compared to the average figure for France of 108 people per km². Almost one in two people live in rural districts.

Between the 1950s and the 1980s, the population of the region declined steadily. Since the mid-1980s however, the overall population has changed little. This hides two important features: first, the contrasts between different parts of the region; and second, the contrasts between natural change and migration.

Most people in the Pyrénées live in small villages or crowded hill-top towns such as Gruissan.

## REGIONAL CONTRASTS

The population of the Pyrénées region in higher, more remote mountain areas is continuing to decline. Traditional small market towns are struggling as they lose their function and jobs. In contrast, the eastern and western fringes are benefiting from urban expansion, the growth of tourism and the increase in retirement homes. Other pockets of increase are developing in the districts around Toulouse, which is the centre of good transport routes. In some mountain valleys associated with tourism activities, such as winter skiing and summer walking, there are signs that the population is recovering.

## NATURAL CHANGE AND MIGRATION

Between 1988 and 1998, across all six departments of the Pyrénées, more people moved in than moved out. However, all had natural decreases (more deaths than births each year due to low birth rates). Therefore, the increase from migration was cancelled out by the rate of natural decrease. The low birth rates have been caused by younger people moving out to seek jobs and improve their lifestyle, while older people move in to retire.

People are moving from the mountains to modern housing such as this development near Biarritz.

## CASE STUDY
### THE PAYS BASQUE

Golfe de Capbreton

Biarritz • • Bayonne

COASTAL ZONE

HILL ZONE

SPAIN

MOUNTAIN ZONE

N

0      20km
0      15 miles

**KEY TO MAP:**

COASTAL ZONE: Total population (1996): 200,000. Change, 1986–96: 8 per cent growth, concentrated around Bayonne and Biarritz. Age structure is becoming more youthful as younger people move in to take up job opportunities.

HILL ZONE: Total population (1996): 42,000. Change, 1986–96: 2 per cent growth, largely due to land reclamation and modernised agriculture, and to suburban spread from the coastal zone.

MOUNTAIN ZONE: Total population (1996): 15,000. Change, 1986–96: 4.5 per cent decline, caused by natural decrease and net out-migration. A steadily ageing population remains.

Basque townspeople take part in a parade to celebrate the feast of Corpus Christi.

The Basques are a distinctive cultural group with their own language and heritage. The Basque region crosses the France-Spain border at the western end of the Pyrenees mountains. In France, the Pays Basque lies in the Pyrénées-Atlantic department. The Basque people are campaigning for greater political freedom for their communities.

The population of the Pays Basque today is approximately 260,000, although the Basque element makes up less than 50 per cent of this total. Over the past 50 years, the Pays Basque has become increasingly urbanised. In 1956, 42 per cent lived in rural areas; by 1996 this figure had dropped to less than 20 per cent. Between 1986 and 1996, the population increased by more than 15,000, but there has been a continuing shift from the mountains to the coastal zone. The case study on page 29 gives a picture of farming in the hill zone.

# AGRICULTURE

Farming in France is very varied. It is an important part of the national economy.

When you travel through France, it seems a very rural country, which is not surprising when you look at the figures. Almost 60 per cent of France's land area is used for some form of agriculture. France is Europe's largest producer of foodstuffs and provides over 20 per cent of the EU's total output by value. Yet agriculture produces only 3 per cent of the country's Gross Domestic Product (GDP) and provides less than 5 per cent of its jobs.

## A FARMING REVOLUTION

Over the past 30 years, French farming has been modernised and become much more productive. In 1970, French farms produced only two-thirds of the country's needs; by 1995, they produced 130 per cent. France has become the largest exporter of food products in the EU. Between 1970–95, the average farm size doubled from 18–36 hectares, and farms became more specialised. As the farms grew in size, the numbers of farmers and farm-workers dropped from over 3 million to barely 1 million. During the 1990s, the number of farms fell from 900,000–650,000.

Highly mechanised farms of the Paris Basin contrast strongly with small, traditional upland farms.

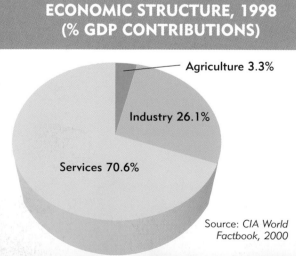

**ECONOMIC STRUCTURE, 1998
(% GDP CONTRIBUTIONS)**

Agriculture 3.3%

Industry 26.1%

Services 70.6%

Source: *CIA World Factbook, 2000*

## COMMON AGRICULTURAL POLICY (CAP)

The modernisation of French farming has been helped greatly by the Common Agricultural Policy (CAP) of the EU, which helped farmers, especially in poorer regions. However, this policy brought major changes to rural environments, including the creation of larger fields and modern buildings for intensive production. Changes to the CAP, such as the introduction of milk quotas in 1984 to limit production and the reduction of support prices (subsidies that guarantee prices) in 1992, have slowed down growth. In recent years, some products, such as wine and milk, have been declining.

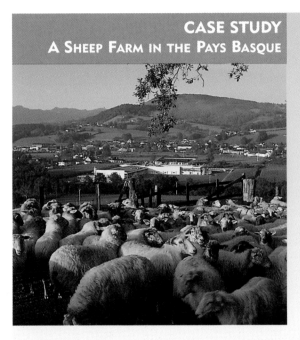

### CASE STUDY
### A SHEEP FARM IN THE PAYS BASQUE

Paul Buchon prepares to move his flock to a fresh pasture.

Paul Buchon's farm lies in the hill zone of the Pays Basque, in south-west France. His farm buildings are on the edge of the village and his 32 hectares are nearby, in two blocks running up the valley sides. The average farm size in the Pays Basque hills is 24 hectares.

Sheep are the main livestock of Basque agriculture, with a total of over ½ million animals. Paul, like most of his neighbours, is a sheep farmer, with a flock of 180 animals. This is larger than the local average of 150 sheep. The climate is mild enough for them to graze outside all year, although he does have a lambing and shearing pen at the farm. Over 80 per cent of Paul's land is permanently covered by grass. The remaining 6 hectares or so he usually plants with maize, which he cuts for silage and winter forage. He keeps a dairy cow to supply his family with milk.

Some lambs are fattened and sold for meat, but the main products of the flock are wool and milk. This is the region of cheeses such as Roquefort and Chaume, made with sheep's milk. Paul is a member of a marketing cooperative, which organises the collection and processing of the milk. There is a similar organisation for the wool fleeces. He and his son run the farm, with a part-time worker to help with the milking. During the spring shearing, additional workers are hired.

When asked what has changed on the farm, Paul said: "To get the best from the CAP and to meet the quality regulations, I've made three main changes since I took over from my father in 1975. First, I've bought an extra ten hectares. This was not difficult, since local farmers sell up when they retire, so there are fewer people in the valley now. Farms around here are steadily getting bigger. Second, I've specialised and become more productive. My sheep have always been most important but, like most of my neighbours, I used to raise a few beef cattle and pigs, and grow patches of wheat. Now I have a larger flock, plant only maize for feed and get much higher yields and quality from my sheep. Third, I have modernised my methods. I used to have two more workers, but now I have a tractor, silage maker, modern shearing pen and milk storage equipment. I know that because there are fewer jobs in farming, young people move away. But I have to change with the times to make a living."

Vineyards in Languedoc-Roussillon.

A modern dairy farm in Brittany.

# REGIONAL PATTERNS

One of the most important features of French farming is its diversity. This makes it difficult to divide France into agricultural regions. Yet, as you travel the country, a number of regional patterns do emerge. In general, there is more arable land in the north, with grassland increasing towards the southern and eastern regions.

France can be divided into five regional types of agriculture, based on the dominant agricultural products. These large regions are very generalised and there is great local variation within each region. For example, the 'mainly animal rearing' region includes both intensive beef cattle rearing on the fertile land of Normandy and extensive sheep grazing on the poor soils of the Massif Central. Vines are grown widely within the mixed farming region and may even be locally dominant, for example in the Burgundy districts north of Dijon.

There are also important regional variations in average farm size. In general, farms are larger in the mainly arable regions such as the Paris Basin, and smaller in upland and southern regions, such as the vine and vegetable-growing districts of Provence, and the sheep-grazing communities of the Pays Basque of south-west France. Despite the growth of farms in recent years, there are still traditional, small family holdings in many areas. However, commercial pressures are causing increasing problems for traditional communities (see case study opposite).

## TOP AGRICULTURAL PRODUCTS BY VALUE, 1998

|  | Percentage of national total |
| --- | --- |
| 1. Milk | 16% |
| 2. Cereals | 14.5% |
| 3. Wine & grapes | 14% |
| 4. Beef cattle | 12% |

Source: *CIA World Factbook, 2000*

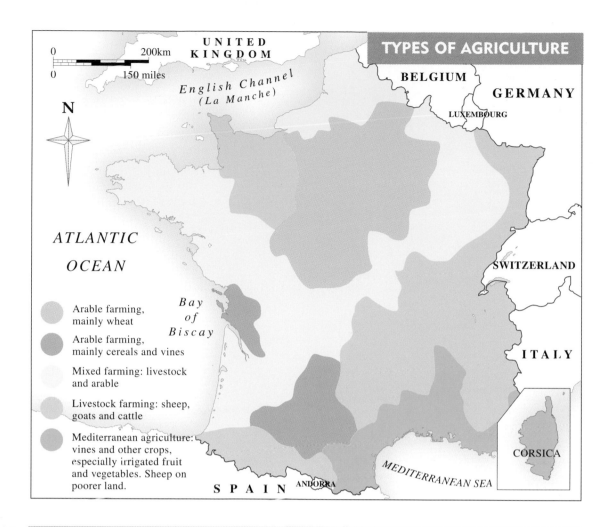

0  200km

0  150 miles

N

UNITED KINGDOM

English Channel (La Manche)

BELGIUM

GERMANY

LUXEMBOURG

ATLANTIC

OCEAN

SWITZERLAND

Bay of Biscay

Arable farming, mainly wheat

Arable farming, mainly cereals and vines

Mixed farming: livestock and arable

Livestock farming: sheep, goats and cattle

Mediterranean agriculture: vines and other crops, especially irrigated fruit and vegetables. Sheep on poorer land.

ITALY

CORSICA

SPAIN   ANDORRA

MEDITERRANEAN SEA

## CASE STUDY
### FIGHTING GLOBALISATION IN LANGUEDOC

The following newspaper extract shows an example of commercial pressures on the traditional community of Aniane, a village in Languedoc-Roussillon:

From *The Guardian*, 18 May 2001

'The Californian winemaking giant Robert Mondavi has pulled out of a unique project to produce high-class red wines in southern France. The Mondavi winery had reached an agreement to turn 50 hectares of virgin wooded hillside, belonging to the village of Aniane, into a vineyard producing a top-quality Languedoc wine. The company planned to invest £5.5 million in preparing and planting the land, modernising Aniane's antiquated wine cooperative, building new, hi-tech storage facilities and, in conjunction with 25 local growers, producing and promoting the 240,000 bottles a year the venture would have produced.

Mondavi's project was initially welcomed last year by the village council, regional authorities and most local growers, who all saw it as a chance to boost the generally poor image of Languedoc wines and establish a genuine international profile. But local environmentalists and the powerful hunting lobby objected. They claimed the plan would destroy the unique ecologocial heritage of the unspoiled l'Arboussas hillside outside Aniane, as well as creating a powerful competitor to the region's winegrowers, most of whom worked on small vineyards.'

## BRITTANY: A FARMING SUCCESS STORY

Until the 1970s, Brittany was a region of small, traditional farms and a declining rural economy. The only thriving sector was the supply of early-season fresh vegetables for urban markets. Today, the five departments of north-west France have become one of the country's wealthiest agricultural regions.

By 1997, Brittany was producing 14 per cent of the total national farming output by value from only 6 per cent of the agricultural area. It was the country's top-producing region for livestock products, and grew 25 per cent of France's fresh vegetables. This remarkable change has been helped by financial support from two main sources: grants and subsidies from the CAP of the EU; and investments by the French government as part of their strong planning policies aimed at regenerating declining regions.

The main results of the financial support have been:

- Improved road and rail infrastructure, giving better access to the cities.
- Modern food-processing plants and abattoirs, raising the quality and scale of production.

ABOVE: Intensive chicken farming in Brittany. These chickens are being reared for their meat.

INSET: Eggs from an intensive battery farm are prepared for transport to urban markets.

- District cooperatives have been set up to improve the standards of marketing.
- Older farmers have been given financial help to retire, which makes land available to create larger farms.
- Bigger fields have been grouped into larger, more efficient blocks.
- A greater use of fodder crops, particularly maize, to increase animal productivity.
- Greater investment in greenhouses, plastic tunnels and irrigation systems by the market gardeners of the northern and southern fringes of Brittany.

*Rice fields and drainage channels in the Camargue.*

The specialisation of farms has been an important feature in the modernisation of French agriculture. However, for some areas, modernising has meant the opposite trend: diversification. The Mediterranean coastlands are good examples.

Forty years ago, the coastal plain of Languedoc-Roussillon was one of France's poorest areas. Farms were small (mostly less than 5 hectares), fragmented, and heavily dependent on vines that gave low-quality wine. In some districts, vines had become a form of monoculture. With CAP and French government support, the area of vines has been reduced, the quality of grapes improved and new crops introduced. Canals and pipeline systems have been built to supply irrigation water. The water and the mild climate allow the growth of a wide range of soft fruits, orchard fruits and vegetables. The small, fragmented holdings are still a problem, but cooperatives have been formed to make buying, selling and marketing more efficient. *Autoroutes* (motorways) provide access to large urban markets throughout France. Vines remain very important and the region produces 30 per cent of France's wine, but the landscape has been transformed.

The Rhône delta, known as the Camargue, is a wetland where the main farming has traditionally been cattle grazing. Large-scale drainage schemes have allowed extensive rice growing and improved grazing pastures. The sheep farmers of the Garrigues hills, on the edge of the coastal plain, traditionally moved their flocks to the rugged Cévennes during the summer. Now, increasing numbers of them are using the Camargue pastures instead.

These changes have had a damaging effect on the environment. Biodiversity has been reduced by the removal of hedges, trees and permanent grass meadows, and the increased use of agrochemicals. The increase in arable land and the removal of hedge and tree cover means that rainwater runs off more quickly into the streams. This increases the likelihood of flooding. The intensification of farming has caused problems of water pollution, as farmyard slurry and chemicals have entered the groundwater and streams. Urban growth has taken up agricultural land. For example, the intensive market-gardening districts around Nantes, in southern Brittany, are being pushed outwards as the city expands.

# INDUSTRY

Massive oil terminals and refineries at Fos, near Marseille.

France is one of the leading industrial countries of the EU, along with Germany and the UK. Approximately 25 million people are in the French workforce. As in all developed countries, jobs have been moving away from agriculture and manufacturing towards service industries. The industrial sector providing the highest number of jobs is manufacturing, followed by retail and professional services.

Within the manufacturing sector, the leading types of business are: 1. Food products; 2. Steel and other metals; 3. Electrical and electronic equipment; 4. Transport equipment, including cars; 5. Machinery. These different businesses show that France has a diverse industrial structure typical of a rich, developed country. Yet in the 1990s, unemployment rates were between 10–12 per cent, as a result of problems adjusting to changes in technology, products and markets.

In 1960, most industry was concentrated in a region that stretched from Paris to Strasbourg. There were also clusters between Nantes and St Nazaire (Brittany), Lyon and Grenoble (Rhône-Alpes) and Marseille and Toulon (Mediterranean coast). In addition, most regional cities had specialist industries, such as pottery in Limoges, or vehicle tyres in Clermont-Ferrand. The two most important features were the dominance of the Paris region and the emphasis on traditional heavy industry: coal, iron and steel, shipbuilding, engineering, chemicals and textiles.

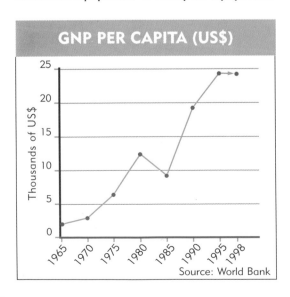

**GNP PER CAPITA (US$)**

Thousands of US$

Source: World Bank

Pouring liquid aluminium into a cast.

By the mid-1980s, 50 per cent of French industry was still located in the Paris Basin, Nord, Lorraine and Rhône-Alpes regions. However, great changes were taking place in structure and location. Seven major changes have taken place over the past 40 years:

1. The decline of the older heavy industries.
2. A shift from manufacturing to an economy led by service industries.
3. Expansion of hi-tech industries such as aerospace.
4. Regional policies aimed at reviving older, declining districts, spreading industrial growth away from Paris.
5. A trend towards larger companies through nationalisation, mergers and more multinational corporations.
6. Increased use of automation and computer systems.
7. A steady increase in the number and proportion of women in paid work.

Old industry in decline: a disused factory near Lille.

# GOVERNMENT POLICIES

In 1970, the French government faced three major economic problems: signs of decline in traditional heavy industries, over-concentration around Paris, and under-development in western and southern France. To tackle these problems, the two main policies of the French government have been regional development and nationalisation.

## DEVELOPING THE REGIONS

Most regional development has been through the creation of growth poles. These are existing cities which have become centres of regional growth, encouraged by government and EU funding (see map opposite). Their French name is *metropoles d'equilibre* meaning 'centres of balance', because they are meant to provide greater geographical balance to reduce the dominance of Paris.

The most successful growth poles are Rennes, Nantes and St Nazaire in Brittany; Toulouse in Aquitaine; Lyon, St Etienne and Grenoble in Rhône-Alpes; and Marseille and Fos on the Mediterranean coast. Each city has achieved at least 30 per cent growth over the past 30 years. The shift of the car industry away from Paris has helped Rennes and Lyon. Some of the growth has been based on modernising well-established industries, for example the building of port facilities at Fos. This has attracted oil refineries, chemical plants and steelworks. In other cases, hi-tech industries have been attracted. For example, Marseille is the base for 25 telecommunications companies and is a hub for southern Europe. In central Marseille, the *Euromediterraneé* redevelopment project consists of over 300 hectares of offices, business parks, hotels and housing.

## HI-TECH AND SERVICE INDUSTRIES

The most impressive recent industrial growth has been where hi-tech and service industries have been attracted. For example, the success of Toulouse is based on aerospace and research. It is the home of Airbus. Lyon and Grenoble have used their high-quality environments to attract electronics firms,

The Technopolis Science Park in Grenoble, a centre for hi-tech companies in an attractive environment.

financial service businesses, research and development (R & D) facilities, often attached to universities. For example, Renault (vehicles), Rhône Poulenc (pharmaceuticals), Elf (oil) and Thomson (electronics) are all major corporations with R & D activities in the region. Many of these hi-tech industries are in science parks (known as *technopoles*) in attractive environments. Science parks are a feature of growth in many parts of France. Despite this recent growth, however, two-thirds of all R & D activities are still found in the Paris region, and Paris remains the largest, single industrial centre in France.

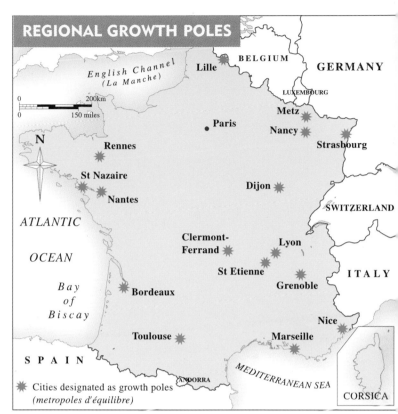

**REGIONAL GROWTH POLES**

English Channel (La Manche)

BELGIUM
GERMANY
LUXEMBOURG

Lille

Paris

Metz
Nancy
Strasbourg

N

Rennes

St Nazaire

Nantes

Dijon

SWITZERLAND

ATLANTIC

OCEAN

Clermont-Ferrand

Lyon

St Etienne

Grenoble

ITALY

Bay of Biscay

Bordeaux

Nice

Toulouse

Marseille

SPAIN

ANDORRA

MEDITERRANEAN SEA

CORSICA

✳ Cities designated as growth poles (*metropoles d'équilibre*)

Modern office buildings and open-air cafés reflect the prosperity of Lyon.

## DECLINE AND REJUVENATION

Growth poles in older, declining industrial regions such as Nord and Lorraine have been less successful than the south. Unemployment levels are so high that jobs created by new industries, such as the BMW factory at Arras, light assembly industries and service industries, have not been enough.

Yet there have been successful projects, such as the port developments at Dunkerque and regeneration in Lille. There has been some success too, in bringing new industries to cities dominated by single companies (see the Clermont-Ferrand case study below).

## CASE STUDY
### CLERMONT-FERRAND: A REGIONAL GROWTH POLE

Clermont-Ferrand lies at the northern edge of the Massif Central. For centuries it has been an important market town for the Auvergne region. During the twentieth century it became an industrial city of 350,000 people, based around the growth of the Michelin company. In 1914, Michelin was a family firm with 5,000 workers. By 1985, it had 30,000 employees and helped to provide one-in-three jobs in Clermont-Ferrand. By 1997, the number of employees had fallen to 20,000, but Michelin is still the city's largest employer.

In contrast to the city, the surrounding Auvergne region has been losing population. In 1964, Clermont-Ferrant was named as a growth pole to improve the economy of the region. Being a growth pole has also helped the city as Michelin employed fewer people. A telecommunications firm and a pharmaceutical firm each employ more than 1,500 people.

The greatest growth has been in service industries which, by 1997, provided more than 70,000 jobs. There is a wide range of activities, including publishing, advertising, retailing, research and administration. This widens the region's range of industries and makes it less dependent on the Michelin company. The growth pole's influence extends at least 50km beyond the main city. Roads have been improved, there is a new airport, and businesses have been set up in surrounding towns and villages. There is increased investment and earnings.

The Michelin corporation is the largest employer in Clermont-Ferrand.

## CASE STUDY
### REVIVING THE NORD REGION

Modern deep-water harbour facilities at Dunkerque, part of the Nord region's regeneration policy.

Fifty years ago, the Nord/Pas-de-Calais region was the centre of heavy industry in France. Its growth had been based on local coal and iron ore resources, and a tradition of textiles. The main industries were coal, iron and steel, metal products, chemicals and textiles. In 1950, the region produced almost 30 million tonnes of coal; in 1991, the last mine closed. In the 1970s, 10,000 jobs were lost in the steel industry. In 1950, over 100,000 people worked in the textile industry; by 1998 there were only 20,000. Overall, between 1970 and 1990, one-third of industrial jobs were lost. In many districts more than 20 per cent of workers were unemployed. Population declined as people moved away.

The government, with EU support, has made great efforts to revive the region in the following ways:
- Improving the road, rail and air transport systems. The aim is to improve the region's accessibility to the rest of France and to take advantage of its location close to other EU countries.
- Modernising existing industries. For example, from 1970, new deep-water port facilities were built at Dunkerque to allow the development of modern steelworks and chemical plants.
- Attracting new industries by offering financial help and few planning restrictions. For example, during the 1980s, Peugeot was persuaded to locate a factory at Valenciennes, a town badly hit by the closing of coalmines and steelworks. Since 1995, BMW have completed a factory at Arras.
- Making environmental improvements to attract foreign companies and the growing service industries, for example, restoring derelict mining sites and renewing town centres.
- Retraining redundant workers in skills needed in growth industries.

Despite the success of some of these projects, unemployment rates in the region are still above the average for France. Labour costs are high and to survive, textile firms increasingly use factories in North Africa and Eastern Europe because of the cheap labour.

## THE INTERNATIONAL EFFECT

There is an important international element in French industrial growth, which works in three ways:

1. French companies selling and located across the world, for example Renault, which controls Nissan (Japan), Elf and Michelin.
2. French companies working on joint projects with foreign companies. For example, Airbus assembles aircraft in Toulouse, with parts made in the UK, Germany, the Netherlands, Spain and elsewhere in France.
3. Investment in France by foreign companies. For example, in 1997, 28 multinational corporations had their office headquarters in Paris, making Paris the third-favourite city for company headquarters after Tokyo and London. Ford has plants at Charleville (Nord) and Bordeaux (Aquitaine). Fiat has 13 components factories scattered across the country. Sony is in Bayonne and Dax in south-west France.

These are all examples of globalisation at work. All major industries and employers in

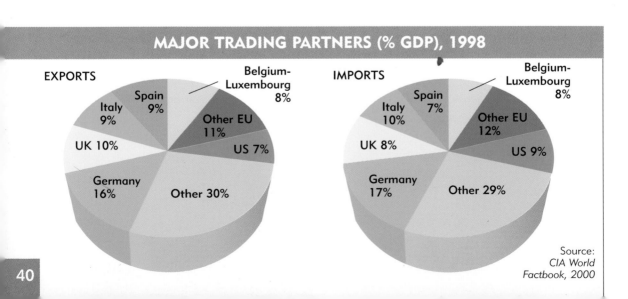

## MAJOR TRADING PARTNERS (% GDP), 1998

**EXPORTS**
- Spain 9%
- Italy 9%
- UK 10%
- Germany 16%
- Other 30%
- US 7%
- Other EU 11%
- Belgium-Luxembourg 8%

**IMPORTS**
- Spain 7%
- Italy 10%
- UK 8%
- Germany 17%
- Other 29%
- US 9%
- Other EU 12%
- Belgium-Luxembourg 8%

Source: CIA World Factbook, 2000

Part of the huge Airbus aircraft assembly complex at Toulouse.

France are now part of the global economy, as well as the EU economy. The benefits include large-scale production and access to larger markets. The dangers include being at risk from decisions taken far away.

## THE NATIONALISATION AND PARTNERSHIP APPROACH

Nationalisation is the process where a government takes control of a company or an industry. The main reason why the French government introduced nationalisation, especially during the 1970s and 1980s, was to modernise key industries and make them more competitive. The coal and energy industries, railways, iron and steel and the motor industry have all been under government control at some time during the past 30 years.

As the EU has become stronger, the French government has shifted from nationalisation towards a partnership policy with private companies. So, as in much of the EU, during the 1990s there was a swing back to private ownership. However, in order to keep some control in industries important for the economy of France, the government still owns part of major companies and acts as a partner in the business. For example in 2001, it was a part-owner of Elf (oil), Renault (vehicles), SNCF (railways) and Airbus (aerospace).

The iron and steel industry is a good example of how nationalisation has worked. In the 1970s, France had too many steelworks. Costs were high and the products were not competitive. The government encouraged companies to merge. By 1980, 80 per cent of French steel was produced by two large groups (Usinor and Sacilor). Then the industry was nationalised. Output was concentrated on a few large, modern steelworks, for example Dunkerque in the north, Fos in the south and two plants in Lorraine. Between 1975–95, the numbers employed fell from 150,000–15,000. In contrast, output fell much less, from 15.5–13.5 million tonnes. Today the industry is more efficient and the government has become only a part owner.

The modern Renault car factory in the Paris suburbs, which replaced an older factory in the inner city.

# LEISURE AND TOURISM

Beaches, mountains, forests and lakes attract millions of tourists to France each year.

France is the world's leading tourism destination. In 1999, over 69 million foreign tourists arrived and there were 65 million day-excursion visits. This was an increase of 80 per cent from 1987. In addition, French people take more than 160 million leisure trips within France each year.

Tourist attractions include high-profile sports events such as the 1992 Winter Olympics, and the 1998 Football World Cup. Each year, the Tour de France cycle race is the biggest national sporting event. Even small communities have their own sports halls, hard-surface tracks, pitches and courts. Leisure and tourism raise approximately US$25 billion a year, which is 7 per cent of the country's GDP. One in ten jobs is associated with leisure and tourism, and tourism is now one of France's most important industries.

France's popularity as a tourist destination is not surprising. It is easily accessible from many European countries and its culture is famous worldwide. It has a wide range of natural landscapes, including beaches, mountains, forests and lakes. More than 10 per cent of France is a national park or other type of protected area. The country has beautiful rural landscapes and local cultures, chateaux and historic towns. The major cities

Chateaux and other historic buildings help to attract tourists.

French food and the nation's café culture are famous the world over.

have cultural interests such as cathedrals, museums, galleries and theatres. Over 40 per cent of all holidays are urban-based. France is also famous for its wine and food. Then there are modern attractions such as resorts and theme parks.

## TYPES OF LEISURE

France provides many types of leisure activities, including camping, renting rural cottages, touring in cars, staying in beach resort hotels, walking or skiing in the mountains, and sailing or canoeing on lakes and rivers. As a result, the economic benefits are spread across the country and a wide range of businesses.

The hotel/café/restaurant trade employs 650,000 people, plus another 200,000 seasonal workers. There are at least 20,000 hotels, but they provide only 8 per cent of the accommodation. Campsites provide another 15 per cent. By far the largest type of holiday is staying in one of the 2.8 million holiday homes that are scattered across the country. Most are owned by French families and used for their holidays. Only a minority are rented out. In addition to holidaymakers, people travelling on business account for up to 20 per cent of all spending.

## PROBLEMS AND RISKS

Despite its size and growth, the tourism industry faces some problems. First, it is highly seasonal: almost half of all holidays are taken in July and August. Second, many jobs are low-paid as well as seasonal. Third,

tourism is a 'fashion' industry, which means that destinations and types of holiday risk losing popularity. For example, some older beach resorts are declining in popularity as tourists seek new attractions.

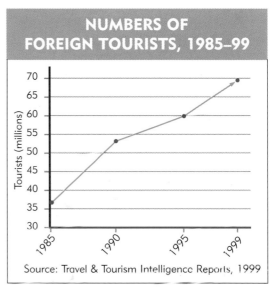

### NUMBERS OF FOREIGN TOURISTS, 1985–99

Source: Travel & Tourism Intelligence Reports, 1999

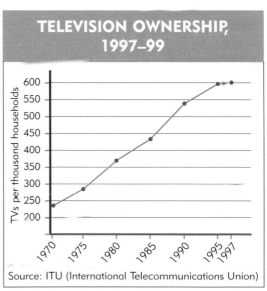

### TELEVISION OWNERSHIP, 1997–99

Source: ITU (International Telecommunications Union)

Disneyland Paris has become the most popular single tourist attraction in France.

## TOURIST ATTRACTIONS, 1998 (MILLIONS OF VISITORS)

### CULTURAL ATTRACTIONS

| | |
|---|---|
| 1. Eiffel Tower, Paris | 5.6 |
| 2. The Louvre galleries, Paris | 5.0 |
| 3. Science City, Paris | 4.0 |
| 4. Palace of Versailles, outside Paris | 3.0 |
| 5. Orsay Museum, Paris | 2.0 |

### THEME PARKS

| | |
|---|---|
| 1. Disneyland Paris | 14.0 |
| 2. Futuroscope, Poitiers | 3.0 |
| 3. Aquaboulevard, Paris | 2.4 |
| 4. Asterix, Plailly | 2.0 |
| 5. Marineland, Antibes | 1.3 |

Source: Tourism Intelligence

## CASE STUDY
### LANGUEDOC-ROUSSILLON

Yachts sail into the port of Gruissan, one of the 'Big Six' tourist resorts.

Languedoc-Roussillon is a region along the Mediterranean coast. Between 1960 and 1975, mass tourism was developed in the region. Six large, planned tourist resorts were built along the coast, linked to the *autoroute* and rail network. Called *unites touristique*, or 'integrated resorts', they are popularly known as the 'Big Six'. Apart from creating wealth in the region, these new resorts have taken pressure off the beautiful holiday destinaton of Provence, which is in danger of over-development and environmental damage. The 'Big Six' resorts have a capacity of more than 200,000 visitors. They supply a wide range of markets and activity types, from camping and apartments to luxury hotels, private villas and exclusive marinas. The majority of owners and visitors are French. There are at least 3 million tourists a year.

# REGIONAL VARIATIONS

Some regions of France attract more tourists than others. The most popular tourist attractions are in the Paris region. The opening of Disneyland Paris in 1992 had a huge impact on tourist numbers. The Disney Corporation chose Paris as the location for their first European theme park because of the fame and image of Paris, and the accessibility from major European markets. Of the visitors to Disneyland Paris, 60 per cent come from outside France.

The seaside is the second main attraction for visitors to France. Seaside resorts are dotted along the French coastline from the English Channel around Brittany, along the Bay of Biscay to the warm shores of the Mediterranean. At least part of most tourists' holidays is spent at the coast.

## TOURISM AND REGIONAL POLICY

The economic development of poorer regions has been an important part of the government's regional planning policies. Several of these poorer regions have attractive environments for visitors, such as Brittany's coastline and rural landscapes; the forests of Vosges; or the remoteness and deep river gorges of the Massif Central. The government has developed tourism facilities and attractions in these regions. Two under-developed areas that have benefited greatly have been the Languedoc-Roussillon coastlands and the French Alps.

## CASE STUDY
### THE FRENCH ALPS

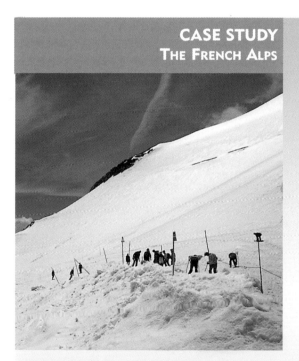

Since 1960, a number of planned resorts have been built to accommodate the increasing number of winter visitors.

By 1960, in many higher, more remote areas of the French Alps, farming was declining and people were leaving. However, skiing was becoming more popular. Local communities and councils took advantage of the sport's popularity and began to install ski facilities, such as pistes and chair lifts. At the same time, the government encouraged the building of a series of specialist ski resorts.

Today, there are two main types of alpine resort. The first are those that have grown around existing farming communities, such as resorts in the Chapelle d'Abondance-Châtel district of Haute-Savoie. The second type are large, high-altitude, high-capacity resorts such as Les Arcs and La Plagne. These have extensive sets of linked cable cars and lifts, plus purpose-built accommodation and services.

During the 1990s the growth of skiing slowed, but in 2000 over 8 million people visited the French Alps for winter sports. Almost 2 million of them were foreign visitors, from countries including the UK and Germany. About 80 per cent of the skiing is concentrated in 15 resorts. Winter sports are high-spending activities, bringing in millions of dollars a year to the region and providing thousands of jobs. The problem of seasonality (visitors concentrated in one season) has become less serious because of the growth of summer activity and touring holidays in the mountains.

Modern apartment blocks in Lyon, typical of many large French cities.

As in all developed countries, the majority of French people live in urban settlements. In 1999, 75 per cent of the population lived in cities. One in three people live in the ten largest urban conurbations (built-up areas that combine several different settlements).

## URBAN GROWTH

Greater Paris has seven times the population of the second-biggest conurbation, Lyon. However, government regional policy has encouraged growth away from the capital. As a result, the highest urban growth rates during the 1990s were in Toulouse, Lyon, Nantes, Toulon and Grenoble. This expansion spilled over to the towns surrounding these cities, in a triangle between Lyon, St Etienne and Grenoble.

## DECLINE AND REGENERATION

In contrast, two types of urban settlement have not grown or have even declined. First there is the network of small market towns, which for centuries have served rural districts. As agriculture has changed, and road transport has increased mobility, these towns have been losing their function. This is especially true for more remote towns and those away from tourist areas.

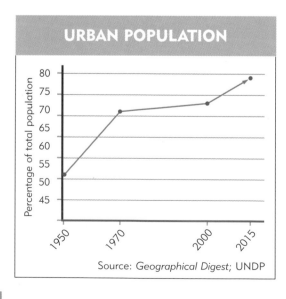

**URBAN POPULATION**

Percentage of total population

80
75
70
65
60
55
50
45

1950  1970  2000  2015

Source: *Geographical Digest*; UNDP

The second group with severe problems has been cities that grew up with traditional heavy industries. For instance, the Lille-Douai-Metz belt of towns and cities in north-east France depended on the textile, chemical, coal and steel industries, which have now declined. Similar problems have arisen in the steel and coal districts around the edges of the Massif Central, such as the town of Le Creusot in the north and Millau in the south.

The French government, with EU support, has introduced policies to revive these older industrial cities. This is called urban regeneration. The aim is to attract new industries, to improve the environmental quality and image of the cities, and to encourage people to live and work there.

| 'TOP TEN' CITIES, 1999 POPULATION | |
| --- | --- |
| Paris | 9.4 million |
| Lyon | 1.4 million |
| Marseille | 1.3 million |
| Lille | 1.0 million |
| Bordeaux | 710,000 |
| Toulouse | 680,000 |
| Nice | 530,000 |
| Nantes | 515,000 |
| Toulon | 450,000 |
| Grenoble | 405,000 |

Source: INSEE 'Statistical Abstract', 1999

## CASE STUDY
### CASTELMORON-SUR-LOT: A STRUGGLING TOWN

The central square of Castelmoron-sur-Lot, lined by old buildings.

Castelmoron-sur-Lot is a small market town that grew up in the Lot valley. In 1996 its population was approximately 1,200, reduced by 1,800 since 1950. Since the mid-1980s, however, its population has remained stable. There is continuing natural decrease (more deaths than births), but this has been balanced by people moving in. The in-migrants are either older people moving into town as they retire, or small numbers of North Africans who work seasonally on local farms.

The town's natural decrease in population is a result of changes in local agriculture. More than 40 per cent of farms in the district have disappeared in the past 30 years. The region's economy is based mainly on rearing livestock. Farms have become more specialised, growing cereals and maize for animal feed, with increased use of irrigation. Yet nearly half of the farms are still less than 10 hectares. Marketing has been improved by the setting up of cooperatives for milk and animals. However, because of greater mobility and economies of scale, much of this buying, selling and processing takes place in larger towns.

Castelmoron's population is 'ageing' as younger people move out and older people stay, or move in when they retire.

# INNER-CITY REGENERATION

The main change in the structure of French cities has been the decline and decay of older, inner-city districts while the suburbs have expanded. People and businesses have been moving outwards. Throughout the 1980s, the inner areas of most French cities were losing their population. During the 1990s however, many had stabilised or were showing slow increases as the result of government regeneration schemes involving housing, jobs and environmental improvements.

Today, inner-city districts tend to have distinctive populations made up of pockets of wealthy people, concentrations of mainly poor immigrant communities, neighbourhoods with high numbers of elderly people and increasing numbers of young adults and single-person households. In 1995, 55 per cent of people aged 15–30 years in inner Grenoble and Lyon had moved in within the past ten years. Unemployment rates are above average in city centres where businesses have moved to the suburbs.

## SUBURBS

The suburbs of many expanding cities are dominated by massive housing projects. These high-density, council developments are mainly clusters of large blocks of flats. A single development may have 50,000 people. Some have become ghettoes, with high concentrations of ethnic minorities and recent immigrants. For example, in the suburbs of Lyon, two projects each have over 40,000 residents. In each, at least two-thirds are of North African origin. This level of segregation has sometimes caused social problems.

A high-density public housing project in the suburbs of Lille.

## CASE STUDY
## REGENERATION IN LILLE

Part of the huge Euralille Centre which is the 'flagship' scheme in the regeneration of Lille.

The Lille conurbation contains three main cities: Lille, Roubaix and Tourcoing. It is one of France's older industrial districts, and its traditional industries of textiles, steel and chemicals, have seriously declined. Between 1975 and 1995, the conurbation lost at least 40,000 manufacturing jobs.

Regeneration schemes have had two aims: first to attract service industries to replace the lost manufacturing businesses; and second to improve the image and attractiveness of the conurbation. The regeneration schemes have had four key elements:

1. The creation of a new town called Villeneuve d'Ascq, on the outskirts of Lille. Begun in 1970, it now contains several universities and research facilities.

2. The building of a modern road and rail system from 1980, making Lille an international transport hub. The key factor has been the routing of TGV (*Train à Grande Vitesse*) rail lines through Lille.

3. The development of the Euralille Centre in central Lille. Begun in 1990 above the TGV station, this large-scale project includes a conference centre, office space, at least 130 shops and cafes, restaurants and apartments. The project has raised the profile and image of Lille as a lively, attractive place to live and work.

4. Improvements to housing quality by the renovation of older, inner-city districts and the upgrading of tower-block estates in the outer suburbs.

Although the population of the Lille conurbation is now increasing slowly, unemployment is still above the national average. Regeneration has been less successful in Roubaix and Tourcoing, where there are still severe problems with poverty, poor-quality housing and derelict industrial land.

# PARIS

In 1999, Paris had a population of 9.4 million, an increase of almost one million since 1975. It is forecast that by 2015, its population will be 11.8 million. The city is the 'powerhouse' of France. It is the centre of national government, the country's principle tourist attraction, the home of major theatres, galleries, museums and universities, and home to one in three foreign residents. The Paris region dominates the rest of France.

## GROWTH POLES

As in other great metropolises, the population of Paris has been spreading outwards from the city centre (see graph page 51). Between 1950–70, a number of new high-density, suburban housing estates built on the outskirts helped this population dispersal. Today, some of these estates have severe problems. Since 1970, the growth has been focused in certain districts of the city, called growth poles. Two of these growth poles, La Défense and Créteil, are massive projects built as business and residential extensions to the main city. Begun in 1957, La Défense today provides 100,000 jobs, accommodation for 31,000 people, the largest shopping complex in the region and conference facilities.

Five other growth poles were new towns built on the outskirts of the city. The new towns absorbed half of all the growth between 1985–95. Marne-la-Vallée is a new town that has benefited from the Disneyland Paris development since 1990. Another growth pole is at Roissy, centred around the expansion of Charles de Gaulle international airport.

## CITY CENTRE

Population density is at its highest in city centres. Despite recent decreases, the Paris city centre is still crowded, with a population density of 245 people per hectare compared with less than 35 per hectare in the outer suburbs. The residential districts of the City of Paris (the central city) are mostly older apartment buildings. The population is very varied, but three distinct groups stand out, each with their own neighbourhoods: the wealthy; the mainly poor, immigrant communities; and young adults, from students to 'yuppies'. Scattered through these neighbourhoods are the elderly, many of whom have lived there most of their lives.

The central areas have changed economically too, with a loss of manufacturing and an increase in professional, financial and commercial businesses. For example, both Citroën and Renault closed old factories in the central zone during the 1980s. Citroën built two new plants in the suburbs and another in Brittany; Renault moved to the suburb of Flins and to the Nord region.

## PARIS FACTS

| | |
|---|---|
| % of France's total land area: | 2% |
| % of French population: | 16% |
| % of French GDP: | 29% |
| Earnings: | 50% above the national average |

The Champs-Elysées, one of the great avenues that make central Paris so famous.

Today almost 75 per cent of the labour force work in service industries: Paris has the largest concentration of such jobs in Europe. Forty per cent of all jobs are still in the city centre of Paris.

## CONGESTION

As the Paris metropolis grows, traffic congestion is becoming more serious. However, massive government investment has

La Défense, the most famous of the huge peripheral housing and business developments in Paris.

transformed the road and rail systems. This improved system helps both internal movements, such as the metro rail network and ring roads, as well as regional connections, such as the TGV lines and *autoroutes* (motorways).

The Ministry of Finance in central Paris is the hub of government.

### THE SPREAD OF PARIS, 1975–95

Population (millions)

| | City centre | Inner suburbs | Outer suburbs | New towns | Outer fringes |
|---|---|---|---|---|---|
| 1995 | 2.3 | 3 | 2.5 | 0.2 | 0.5 |
| 1975 | 2.1 | 2.9 | 2.7 | 0.8 | 1 |

KEY
1995
1975

Source: Noin & White, 1997

# TRANSPORT, ENERGY AND THE ENVIRONMENT

A toll station on an *autoroute* outside Toulouse.

L ike all countries, France is making increasing demands upon its space and resources. The French people are becoming more aware of the impacts of these developments, and a widening range of 'environmental issues' is arising. This section focuses on three important issues: transport, energy and conservation policies.

## TRANSPORT

Transport is an important part of government regional policy in France. Approximately one-third of government money for the regions is spent on transport projects. Paris is the political and business capital of France and by far the largest centre of population, so the priority has been to improve links between Paris and the rest of the country. In addition, to help regional growth, the national plan is that by 2015 every part of France will be within 50km or 45 minutes by car from a motorway, dual carriageway, or rail station on a high-speed line.

### ROADS

The national road network in France is based on a set of motorways (called *autoroutes*) radiating from Paris. Motorways also link the

The TGV high-speed train network is the pride of the French public transport system.

The entrance to the Channel Tunnel at Calais. The tunnel has brought large-scale economic growth to the the region.

regions. By 2000, France had 9,000km of *autoroutes* and traffic increased by 20 per cent during the 1990s. The *autoroutes* are toll roads, which charge a fee for their use. In general, *autoroutes* by-pass central cities. You can now drive all the way across France from Calais to Marseille by *autoroute*.

With high car ownership, traffic congestion in cities is a major problem. Paris is the extreme example. About one-third of commuter trips into the central city are by car and more than 100 million tonnes of goods come and go each year. Despite 800km of motorway, traffic congestion is still severe.

## RAIL

France has built a high-speed rail network for its famous TGV trains (see map on page 9). They travel at up to 300km per hour, with an average speed of 170km per hour. The first TGV line was opened in 1981 and the Channel Tunnel line opened in 1994. In 2001, the 250km stretch of line from Valence to Marseille was completed. You can now travel from Paris to Marseille in just three hours and from Paris to Tarbes in the Pyrenees in six hours. The government has paid for most of the construction and the trains, and still subsidises the system heavily. The TGV lines extend into Belgium, the Netherlands, Germany and Switzerland.

Three TGV lines radiate from Paris, with an important by-pass route linking them. This includes the Charles de Gaulle airport and Disneyland Paris. For travel within Greater Paris, there is the metro system. This covers the central city and the regional railways, which have recently been developed to serve the suburbs and new towns. More than 50 per cent of trips within Greater Paris are on these rail routes. Each day, over 600,000 people commute to central Paris by train. The government subsidises fares by 50 per cent to encourage travel by public transport.

Government subsidies support public transport in all major cities and many have modern systems. For example, in the last 20 years, Lille has built two underground lines with automated trains, and tramway routes linking the city with the nearby towns of Roubaix and Tourcoing.

## AIR

France's two major international airports, Charles de Gaulle and Orly, are both in Paris. Charles de Gaulle is the seventh-busiest airport in the world. Orly, within the built-up area of Paris, is increasingly a hub for internal and European flights. Both are integrated into the *autoroute* and TGV networks.

The government has encouraged the development of regional airports such as Toulouse, Nice, Dijon and Lyon. In some cases, such as with Lyon, the airport connects to the TGV network. However, the speed of *autoroutes* and TGV lines mean that air travel within France may not give quicker total journey times than travelling overland.

# ENERGY

France has taken a distinctive approach to energy generation. In 1966 it completed the installation of the world's first modern tidal power station. This uses the unusually high tidal range of the Rance estuary, in Brittany. The project has been praised for using a renewable energy source (the power of the sea), which is sustainable and does not damage the environment.

The Rance estuary tidal energy station in Brittany harnesses the strong tidal flows through the funnel-shaped estuary.

## HYDROELECTRIC POWER

Hydroelectricity is another sustainable type of energy produced by the power of water. France has built many hydroelectric power (HEP) stations, especially in the mountains of the Rhône-Alpes region. HEP today supplies 13 per cent of France's energy needs. HEP schemes, with their dams and reservoirs, have strong environmental impacts, but they do use a renewable energy source.

## NUCLEAR POWER

The most controversial part of France's energy policy is the use of nuclear energy. In 1978, approximately 13 per cent of the country's total energy came from nuclear power stations. By 1998 the proportion had reached 76 per cent. This is one of the world's highest figures, with only the USA producing more nuclear energy a year. The main aim of using more nuclear power is to make France less dependent on oil and coal imports.

In the mid-1990s, there were 55 nuclear power stations spread across France. Today the main concentrations are in the Loire and Rhône valleys, where there are ample water

## CHANGES IN ENERGY PRODUCTION

|  | Energy Production (gigawatts per hour) | |
|  | 1978 | 1998 |
| --- | --- | --- |
| Fossil fuels (coal, oil, natural gas) | 126 | 54 |
| HEP | 69 | 66 |
| Tidal power | 0.5 | 0.6 |
| Nuclear power | 30 | 388 |
| TOTAL | 225.5 | 508.6 |

Source: INSEE 'Statistical Abstract', 1999

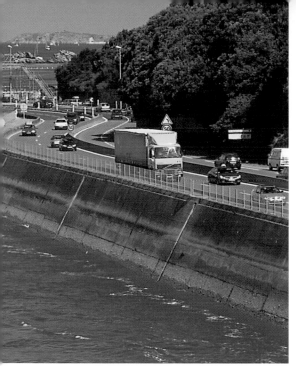

supplies needed by the process of producing nuclear energy. There have been many protests and campaigns against the building of nuclear power stations, for example in Brittany during the 1980s. Campaigners are concerned about the safety of power stations. They believe it could cause a catastrophe if something goes wrong. So far, however, the safety record has been good. A future problem may be the safe decommissioning of older power stations when they are closed down.

## COAL AND GAS

The French coal-mining industry is in serious decline. It now produces less than 5 million tonnes a year, only one third of the output 20 years ago. The country now imports 11 million tonnes of coal a year and uses about 12 million tonnes for generating electricity. Natural gas production from the Pau-Lacq field in the Pyrenees is also declining from its 1980s peak.

Between 1978 and 1998, the total energy production in France more than doubled. France now exports electricity to the UK and other countries. HEP and tidal power production have remained steady, but power from fossil fuels has decreased from 60 per cent to below 11 per cent.

ABOVE: A massive HEP installation at Injoux-Génissiat in the French Alps.

BELOW: France relies more heavily on nuclear power than most countries .

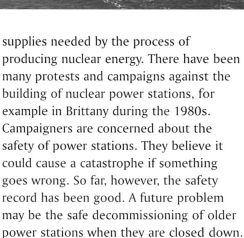

# CONSERVATION

France is changing; its economy is growing, and the French expect an improved quality of life. Modern agriculture, urban growth, new transport routes and tourist travel all have an impact on the environment. It is not surprising therefore, that conservation has become an urgent issue.

Impacts on the environment may be caused by a single activity and be restricted to one locality, such as building a new suburb, or pollution from an oil refinery affecting a stretch of a river. In many cases, however, several causes act together and the effects may be felt at considerable distances. For example, air pollution from cities and industries in Paris and northern France can cause acid rain that damages forests in the Ardennes and the Vosges Mountains. This makes successful conservation difficult.

## CASE STUDY
### PRESSURES ON THE CAMARGUE

The Camargue is the delta of the Rhône River. It covers 500km² and is one of Europe's largest wetlands. These wetlands are important ecosystems. They provide an essential resting place for millions of migrating birds, as well as species that live there all-year-round, such as pink flamingos.

Today, much is changing and pressures are building up from both inside and outside the delta. Internally, canals for navigation, drainage and irrigation criss-cross the delta and about 40 per cent is drained and used for agriculture. Rice and animal grazing fields take up most of the drained land. Roads are being improved and numbers of tourists are increasing. To conserve the remaining natural wetlands and habitats for wildlife, the government has created the 15,000-hectare Camargue Natural Park around the Étang de Vaccarres.

The fragile wetlands of the Camargue are under threat from land drainage, agriculture, tourism and pollution.

Threats from outside the Camargue are more difficult to control. To the west are the large tourist resorts and agricultural lands of Languedoc-Roussillon. Much waste from the resorts is still pumped into the sea. To the east is the huge, urban-industrial sprawl of Marseille and Fos. To the north, water from the Rhône is removed for irrigation along the valley above the delta. There are also increasing risks of water pollution from industrial and agricultural expansion along the Rhône valley from Lyon southwards. The Mediterranean Sea has very small tides, so water pollution is not moved away efficiently.

## CASE STUDY
## SKI RESORTS: THE KNOCK-ON EFFECT

The key natural features of ski resorts are steep slopes, forest vegetation and fast-flowing streams fed by snow-melt and summer storms. When a ski resort is developed, new houses and roads increase the hard surface area, and forest cover is removed to create pistes and lift systems. This allows surface water to run off more quickly and increases soil erosion, which can affect regions far away from the ski resort. Today, there are strict planning controls to reduce the amount of forest that is cut down, to limit the hard surface area and to improve drainage through each resort.

Deforestation in the Val d'Isère - Tigne ski area has increased soil erosion.

# THE FUTURE

The future of France depends on whether the French can continue to improve their quality of life while conserving their environment. Any country faces this challenge, because economic growth and higher standards of living have impacts on the environment. The question is how much and what type of impact are acceptable, and to whom. For example, commuters in Paris want better rail routes, but not too near their homes; villagers in Brittany want reliable, cheap electricity, but oppose a nuclear power station nearby; farmers in the Camargue want to drain more land, and birdwatchers want to keep the wetlands to save the habitat for wildlife.

So environmental issues focus on sustainability. Economic sustainability means making sure there will be jobs in the future. Social sustainability means protecting quality of life for all groups in the population. Environmental sustainability means

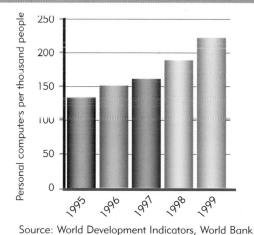

**PERSONAL COMPUTERS**

Personal computers per thousand people

Source: World Development Indicators, World Bank

conserving and improving the quality of environments into the future. As the examples through this book show, it is sometimes difficult to balance all types of sustainability in modern France.

# GLOSSARY

**Agrochemicals** Chemicals used in the agricultural industry.

**Barrage** A structure built across a river to control water levels.

**Biodiversity** The range and number of species in an ecosystem.

**Birth rate** The number of children born in a year per 1,000 population.

**CAP** The Common Agricultural Policy of the European Union (EU). It is the system that provides regulations, advice and financial support for farmers in the countries within the EU.

**Conurbation** Large urban areas created by several towns growing together.

**Cooperative** Where a number of individuals or businesses work together to help each other.

**Crystalline rock** Rocks made up of minerals in a crystalline state.

**Death rate** The number of people who die in a year per 1,000 population.

**Decommissioning** Taking a nuclear power station out of use and dismantling it.

**Diversification** Broadening an economy or business by adding new activities.

**Drainage basin** The total area that contributes water to a river.

**Dredging** Removing sediment from a river bed to maintain a deep channel.

**Economy of scale** The use of mass production to reduce costs and prices.

**Estuary** The mouth of a river where it broadens into the sea.

**EU** The European Union. The group of countries that have joined together to achieve closer political, social, economic and environmental cooperation.

**Extruded** Material pushed to the earth's surface by heat and pressure from below.

**Fault** A line or zone caused by the breaking or shearing of rocks as a result of enormous forces.

**Fertility rate** The average number of children a woman gives birth to during her lifetime.

**Fodder crop** A crop grown to be fed to animals.

**Fold mountains** Mountains created by the bending or flexing of rocks caused by enormous compressing forces.

**Ghetto** An urban district containing a high proportion of one ethnic or cultural group.

**Growth pole** A city chosen by the government to be a focus for economic expansion.

**Hinterland** The area around a city that comes under its economic and social influence.

**Infrastructure** The transport, communication and services (water, electricity, sewerage, etc) networks and systems that support an economy and society.

**Intensification** Farming more intensively to make the land produce more crops or other plant food.

**Irrigation** The controlled addition of water to the land to improve plant growth.

**Meander** A loop-like bend in a river.

**Monoculture** Concentrating on a single product on a farm.

**Natural increase** The excess of births over deaths.

**Plateau** A relatively flat-topped upland.

**Population structure** The numbers and proportion of people in particular age-groups within a population.

**Precipitation** A general term for rain, hail and snow.

**Productivity** The amount of output achieved from a certain level of resource use, investment and effort.

**Quality of life** The level of economic, social and environmental satisfaction experienced by a person or community.

**Refugee** A migrant who has been forced to flee from his/her home country.

**Regeneration** The process of reviving a declining area.

**Replacement level** The minimum number of children a woman needs to have if a population is not to decline in the future.

**Sedimentary rock** Layers of rock formed from sediments carried by water, ice or wind, that are then deposited and slowly solidified over a long period of time.

**Segregation** Where different social, ethnic and cultural groups live in separate residential areas.

**Slurry** A muddy mixture of solid and liquid material.

**Specialisation** The concentration on one or a number of products or services.

**Subsidy** A contribution of money, especially one made by a government to support a project.

**Terrace** The gently sloping remains of an earlier river floodplain.

**Tidal range** The difference in sea level between high and low tides.

**Tributary** A stream or river that flows into the main channel of a river.

# FURTHER INFORMATION

## BOOKS TO READ:

*The Blue Guide for France* by I. Robertson (Black, latest edition) This national 'Blue Guide' gives very useful background information on regions and localities. There is also a set of regional 'Blue Guides', which will support regional case studies.

*Contemporary Europe: A geographic analysis* by W.H. Berentsen (Wiley & Sons, 1997) Reference book with chapters on topics such as agriculture, industry and countries, including France.

*Contemporary France* by H.P.M. Winchester (Longman, 1994) A source for more detail on topics covered in this book.

*Country Fact Files: France* by Veronique Bussolin (Hodder Wayland, 1994) Illustrated reference for KS2–3.

*Country Studies: France* by Celia Tidmarsh (Heinemann Library, 1999) Illustrated reference for KS4.

*Eurostat Yearbook, 2001* (Eurostat DG XXIII; Luxembourg Office for the Official Publications of the European Commission, 1997) A detailed data source for this topic, with a chapter on France. Eurostat is a useful source of information on France and other EU countries.

*Exploring France* by Peter Wickert (Hodder & Stoughton Educational, 1999) In-depth study of France for KS3 and foundation GCSE level.

*Exploring France Mapcards* by Vincent Bunce (Hodder & Stoughton Educational, 1997) A set of mapcards containing an atlas-style map of France and detailed graphical and statistical data.

*Foundation History: the French Revolution* by David Taylor (Heinemann Educational Secondary Division, 1997) Textbook for KS4/GCSE.

*France and the World Since 1870* by John Keiger (Arnold, 2001) Relations between France and the rest of the world over the twentieth century.

*France in Revolution* by Duncan Townson & Dylan Rees (Hodder & Stoughton Educational, 2001) Examines the causes, course and impact of the French Revolution from its onset to the overthrow of Napoleon.

*The French Revolution, 1789–94* by John D. Clare (Hodder & Stoughton Educational, 2001) Textbook for KS4/GCSE.

*A Geography of the European Union: A regional and economic perspective* by G. Nagle & K. Spencer (OUP, 1996) This book puts France into the EU context. There are chapters covering topics included in GCSE and A-level syllabuses.

*Next Stop: France* by Fred Martin (Heinemann Library, 1997) Illustrated reference for KS2–3.

*The Rough Guide to France* (Rough Guides, 2001) A comprehensive handbook to France, with practical tips and department-by-department commentary.

## WEBSITES:

GENERAL STATISTICS
CIA World Factbook:
http://www.cia.gov/cia/publications/factbook/geos/fr.html

Eurostat: http://europa.eu.int/comm/eurostat/

INSEE: http://www.insee.fr/fr/home/home_page.asp

GENERAL INFORMATION ON FRANCE
French Tourist Office: http://www.franceguide.com
or: www.francetourism.com/

The French Information Centre:
http://www.france.com/

PARIS
http://www.greatestcities.com/paris/paris-6-c.html

# INDEX

Numbers shown in **bold** refer to pages with maps, graphic illustrations or photographs.

agriculture **28–33**, 46, 47, 56 *(see also farming)*
airports 50, 53
Algeria & Algerians 8, **23**, 24 *(see also immigration and migrants)*

Basques **27** *(see also regions: Pays Basque)*
beaches 15, **18**, **42**
birth rate 21, 25, 26

cafés **20**, 43
canals 16, 33, 56
Carmargue 17, **33**, **56** *(see also delta)*
cars 36, **41**, 53 *(see also transport)*
chateaux **42**, 43
children **22**
cities **20**, **21**, 36, **46–51**
  Bordeaux **19**, 41, 47,
  Brittany **32**, 44
  Clermont-Ferrard 34, **38**
  Fos 36, 41
  Grenoble **36**, 46, 47, 48

The Eiffel Tower, Paris.

Le Havre 16
Lille **35**, 38, 47, **48**, **49**
Lyon 24, 36, **37**, **46**, 47, 48
Marseille **19**, 24, 36, 47,
Nantes 36, 46, 47
Nice 47, 53
Paris 20, 44, 46, 47, **50–51**, 52, **60**
Reims 10
Rennes 36
Rouen 16
St Etienne 36, 46
St Nazaire 17
Strasbourg **19**
Toulon 34, 46, 47
Toulouse **20**, **23**, 24, 36, **41**, 46, 47
climate **18–19**, 29, 33 *(see also weather)*
coal 13, 34, 39, 47, 55 *(see also industry and energy)*
coasts **10**, **11**, **12**, **13**, 15, **18**, **33**, 44
colonies 8, 23
Common Agricultural Policy (CAP) 29, 32, 33
conservation **56** *(see also environment and pollution)*
Corsica 8, **9**, 15
culture **9**, 42

dams 17, **54**, **55**
death rate 21, **22**
delta 17, **33**, **56**
Disneyland Paris **44**

energy **54–55**
  hydroelectric 54, **55**
  nuclear 54, **55**
  tidal **54**, 55
environment 33, 39, 44, **56–57** *(see also conservation, erosion and pollution)*
erosion 12, **13**, **14**, **57**
estuaries 16, 17, **54**
Europe 8, 23, **24**, 39, **40** *(see also immigration)*
European Union (EU) 9, 24, 28, 29, 32, 36, 39, 41, 47
export 28, **40**

farms *(see also agriculture)* **28**, **29**, **30**, **32**
  cattle **30**, 33
  intensive 29, 30, **32**, 33
  livestock 32, 47
  mechanised **28**
  sheep **29**, 30, 33
  vegetables 30, 32, 33
  vineyards 30, **31**, 33
fertility rate 22, 25
floods **17**, 33
food 8, **23**, 28, 29, 30, 43

gas 55
glaciers 11, 14
government 8, 20, 32, 33, 36, 39, 41, 46, 47, **51**
Gross Domestic Product (GDP) 8, **28**, **40**, 42
Gross National Product (GNP) **34**
growth poles 36, **37**, **38**, 50

health 22, 25
heritage **8**, 27
holidays, recreation & leisure **18**
housing **21**, 24, **25**, **26**, **46**, **48**, 49, **51**

immigration 8, 22, **23**, **24**, 48 *(see also migration)*
imports **40**
industry 13, 24, **34–41**,
  decline **35**, 36, 38, 46, 49
  heavy 34, 35, 36, **39**, 47, 49
  hi-tech 35, **36**, **37**
  manufacturing 34, 35, **40–41**, 49, 50
  service 34, 35, 36, 38, 39, 49
  tourist **42–45**
inner city 48, 50, **51**
iron ore 13, 39 *(see also industry)*
iron & steel 13, 34, 36, 39, 41, 47 *(see also industry)*
irrigation **33**, 47, 56
jobs 26, **34–41**, 42, 48

Landes **10**, 11, 17
language 8, 27

migration 20, 22, 24, 26, 47 *(see also immigration)*
mountains 10, **14–15**, 43
    Alps 14, **15**, 18, 44, **45**, **55**
    Jura **11**, 13
    Massif Central **11**, **12–13**, 17, 20, 44
    Mt Blanc 8, 14
    Pyrenees **14**, 17, 18, 55
    Vosges **11**, 44
Morocco & Moroccans 8, 23 *(see also immigration and migrants)*
multinationals 35, 40

nationalisation 35, 36, 41

oil **34**, 36 *(see also industry)*

plains 10, **11**
    Aquitaine Basin 10, **11**, 17
    Paris Basin 10, **11**, **28**, 30
pollution 33, 56
population 9, **20–27**, 39, **46**, 50
    density 20, **21**, 26, 50
    structure **25**
ports 16, 38

quality of life 20, 24, 56, 57

rainfall 18–19
regions 8, **9**
    Auvergne **9**, 20
    Bordeaux **9**, **19**

Brittany 9, **12**, **30**, **32**, 33, 34, 36, **54**
Burgundy 9, 30
Languedoc-Roussillon 9, **30**, **31**, **33**, **44**, 56
Limousin 9, 20
Lorraine 9, 13, 38, 41
Midi-Pyrénées 9, **26–27**, 36
Nord 9, 38, **39**
Pays-Basque 9, **27**, **29**, 30
Rhône-Alpes **9**, 20, 34, 35
religion 9
retirement 26, 47
rivers 10, **11**, 12, 13, **16–17**, 43
    Dordogne 17
    Garonne 10, 16, **17**,
    Loire 16
    Rhône 16, **17**, 56
    Seine 10, **16**,

skiing **15**, 26, 43, **45**, **57**
snow 4, **15**, 17, 18, **19**, 57
sport 10, 42, **45** *(see also skiing, walking)*
suburbs 41, 48, 49, 50, **51**

temperature **18–19**
thunderstorms 17, 18
tourism 26, **42–45**, 56 *(see also holidays and recreation & leisure)*
tourist resorts **11**, 43, **44**, 56, **57**

traffic
    barge 16, **17**
    congestion 51, 53
transport *(see also roads and railways)* **52–53**
    air 39, 50, 53
    public transport **52**, 53
    rail 32, 39, 49, 51, **52**, **53**
        TGV 49, 51, **52**, 53
    rivers 26
    road 32, 33, 38, 39, 46, 49, 51, **52**
        *autoroutes* 33, 51, **52**, 53

unemployment 34, 38, 39, 48 *(see also jobs and industry)*
uplands **12–13**
    Ardennes **11**,13
    Brittany Peninsula **11**, **12**, 13

valleys **10**, 12
    Loire 55
    Rhine 10, **11**, 55
    Rhône-Saone 10, **11**, 13, 55
Vietnam 8, 23 *(see also immigration and migrants)*
vineyards 30, **31**, 33 *(see also farms)*

walking **15**, 26, 43
water 16, 17, 33, 56
weather **18** *(see also climate)*
wetlands 11, 17, **33**, **56**
wine 29, **31**, 33, 43

The abbey and village of Mont-Saint-Michel, off the coast of Normandy.